Christmas is a gift

unwrap the significance of the season

PAUL CHAPPELL

First published in 2011 by Striving Together Publications, a ministry of Lancaster Baptist Church, Lancaster, CA 93535. Striving Together Publications is committed to providing tried, trusted, and proven books that will further equip local churches to carry out the Great Commission. Your comments and suggestions are valued.

Striving Together Publications
4020 E. Lancaster Blvd.
Lancaster, CA 93535
(800) 201-7748

Cover design by Andrew Jones
Layout by Craig Parker
Edited by Monica Bass

ISBN 978-1-59894-184-5
Printed in the United States of America

Contents

Introduction
GOD'S WRAPPING PAPER

Remember the first Christmas gifts your children gave you—the ones when they were old enough to understand what they were doing? Remember their relentless insistence on wrapping the gifts themselves? My children encased their first gifts to me in enough Scotch tape to wrap ten or twenty gifts! The paper underneath was usually wrinkled and torn—evidence of their multiple attempts to get it just right. But the gifts were wrapped in love, and they were a joy to my heart.

A wrapped gift allows the recipient the joy of discovery. Sure, we could just toss a pile of toys under the tree for our kids, but it's more fun for them to anticipate and discover—one corner at a time—what is underneath the gift wrap.

One study revealed that each year Americans use over 38,000 miles of ribbon to wrap their Christmas presents. The presents themselves are covered in four million tons of wrapping paper and gift bags. Apparently, we like wrapping gifts.

Or maybe we like *un*wrapping them.

Christmas is the kind of gift we can unwrap for our entire lifetime and still not completely discover God's infinite love.

Usually we think of Christmas as an event, and what an event it was! Jesus came to Earth over two thousand years ago. He was born of a virgin and laid in a manger where He was heralded by angels and worshipped by shepherds. That was the first Christmas.

But Christmas is more than an event. It is a gift. Through Christmas, we can experience God's presence, know His peace, and live with His continual joy.

Best of all, Christmas is a gift with *your* name on it. It is God's love personally delivered through Christ to *you*.

Christmas often finds us consumed with the details of planning, shopping, and wrapping gifts for others. From the children's school parties, to the gift exchange at work, to the family celebration, the month of December is brimming with gift preparation—for others. If we're not careful, in the rush of Christmas we miss enjoying God's gift to *us*.

I'd like to encourage you to make some time this Christmas to unwrap *your* gift—to discover the love God sent to *you* in the form of a tiny baby.

My prayer is that this book will help you discover the difference the gift of Christmas can make in your life all year long. This Christmas, discover—or rediscover—the gift that is specially and perfectly yours—Christmas itself.

CHAPTER ONE

Emmanuel
THE GIFT OF HIS PRESENCE

Carter, a young boy, sat down at the kitchen table to write a letter to God about the Christmas presents he especially wanted. "I've been good for six months now," he began. He paused in thought and then crossed out the "six months" and wrote "three months" in its place. Again he hesitated. Then he marked out "three months" and wrote "two weeks." Finally, he put his pencil down and walked into the living room. He stood in front of the wooden nativity set on the coffee table, picked up the figure of Mary, and then returned to his letter. "Dear God," he wrote, "If you ever want to see your mother again…."

We smile at Carter's attempt to manipulate because we know it was an empty threat. The small statue of Mary that Carter abducted was just a figurine. But we are only too prone to likewise reduce the players in the Christmas story—especially the Baby—to a set of figurines.

Consider for a moment the significance of the tiny baby in the manger. It represents the very presence of God. As the angel told Joseph, His name is Emmanuel: God with us (Matthew 1:23).

Christmas is a gift—the gift of Christ's presence.

Have you ever stopped to consider what life would be like *without* Christ's presence? What if Jesus had never come?

One of my favorite Christmas traditions while our children were still at home was watching "It's a Wonderful Life" together. Ideally, we would do it the same evening we set up the electric train in the living room. With cups of hot cocoa and bowls of popcorn, we enjoyed our Christmas family time.

If you've never seen this movie, I'll summarize it for you: George Baily, the main character, found himself in a deep financial hole at Christmas time. It seemed the harder he worked to provide for his family and the more he gave to others, the deeper he sunk. In desperation, George decided he was a failure and wished he had never been born. In fact, he drove to a bridge and prepared to take his own life.

Just in time, Angel Second Class Clarence Oddbody (yes, I know the movie isn't theologically sound) enters the scene. Clarence grants George his wish of never being born and then shows George what the lives of others would have been like without George. In the end, George discovers that his seemingly insignificant life had actually made a profound difference in his family and even the entire town.

George learned that one person can make an enormous difference in the lives of others. I'm sure you can think of people who have made a significant difference in your life—a friend, a family member, a teacher, a coach, a coworker, a neighbor. Whether you knew them well or were helped by their example from a distance, their presence and influence changed your life.

If a single human can have this much impact on us, consider again: what if *Jesus* had never come? The difference His presence can make in our lives is indispensable…and incomprehensible.

GOD WITH US

There's no question that the arrival of a new baby changes everything. One very little person has a way of taking control of an entire family! When Baby arrives, life (and usually sleep!) is altered for everyone.

I'll never forget the joy of welcoming each of our four children into the world. When our oldest, Danielle, was born, she not only changed life for us, but my wife teases me about how I changed life for others. Believe it or not, I actually made the visitors who came to our home wear a gown and mask when they wanted to hold our baby. (By the time our first grandson came along, I had softened my germ-conscious enforcements so that I required people only to wash their hands immediately before holding him.)

Sanitation procedures aside, there is nothing that reminds us of the miracle of birth like holding a newborn baby. As I held each of our four children and, years later, our two grandchildren for the first time, I couldn't help but marvel at the wonder of a newly created life.

But Jesus' birth was a miracle for another reason. In fact, not only was His *birth* a miracle, but consider His *conception*. Because Jesus is God, He could not be conceived through the natural process as other men. And that is why one day, in the small town of Nazareth, a young Hebrew girl received a surprise visitor.

Mary was actually the first to learn of Jesus' impending arrival. She was betrothed to a young man named Joseph and was, no doubt, happily looking forward to marriage.

But Mary's world was forever changed the day Gabriel visited her. There was no forewarning, no indication she would receive an angelic messenger; he just suddenly appeared. "Hail, thou that art highly favoured," he greeted, "the Lord is with thee: blessed art thou among women" (Luke 1:28).

Talk about startled. More like rattled! I'm quite certain Mary hadn't prepared for a visit from Heaven that day. And she especially hadn't prepared for the news the angel brought. No wonder she was "troubled at his saying, and cast in her mind what manner of salutation this should be" (Luke 1:29).

But Gabriel had more to say:

> *Fear not, Mary: for thou hast found favour with God. And, behold, thou shalt conceive in thy womb, and bring forth a son, and shalt call his name JESUS. He shall be great, and shall be called the Son of the Highest: and the Lord God shall give unto him the throne of his father David: And he shall reign over the house of Jacob for ever; and of his kingdom there shall be no end.*—LUKE 1:30–33

I can imagine Mary pausing to absorb what she had just heard and experienced. Of all things, an angel from Heaven had just visited her. And what had he announced?

God is coming to Earth. And He is entering the world through my womb.

Pause with Mary to absorb the significance of Gabriel's announcement. God Himself is taking on flesh and coming to live among us. As Charles Spurgeon wrote, "He who never began to be, but eternally existed, began to be what He eternally was not, and continued to be what He eternally was."

Emmanuel—God with us. What does it mean?

HE UNDERSTANDS US

When we unwrap the significance of this gift—God with us—we realize that we can never again accuse God of misunderstanding us or our circumstances.

> *The wonder of it all,*
> *That in a manger stall*
> *That night in Bethlehem,*
> *God became a man!*

One of us,
The Holy Child was born,
He became one of us
On Christmas morning!
—AUTHOR UNKNOWN

When my son Larry was younger, I took him outside one day to teach him how to play basketball. I would shoot and show him the techniques, then hand him the ball. He was still fairly young, and he struggled to get the ball to the rim. Finally, after I made another shot, Larry said, "Yeah, Dad, it's easy for you up there, but you don't know what it's like from down here!"

He had a good point.

Sometimes we repeat Larry's words to our Heavenly Father. "God, it's easy for You to say what we should do and what we should be, but You don't know what these circumstances are like from down here!"

Christmas proves otherwise.

And the Word was made flesh, and dwelt among
us, (and we beheld his glory, the glory as of the

only begotten of the Father,) full of grace and truth.
—JOHN 1:14

God *does* know what it is like for us down here. He came in person, wrapped in a tiny human body. He lived among us, experiencing human life from our perspective and through our limitations. He knows the trials we go through; He understands the pressures we feel. He is Emmanuel—God with us.

Have you ever longed for someone who could understand how you feel? Someone who has experienced what you are going through?

Jesus is that Someone.

Jesus experienced the pressures of living in a sin-cursed world. He felt the full gamut of human emotions—including rejection, loss, grief, and heartache, as well as joy, encouragement, and victory. He knew the harsh realities of government oppression and felt the strain of poverty. He knew obscurity and painful popularity. He ate, slept, walked, talked, and interacted with others. And, not to contradict the author of "Away in a Manger," but as a baby, He even cried. He needed care. He grew. He built relationships. In short, He lived what we experience. He became "one of us."

Obviously then, Christ can give divine empathy in our burdens and struggles. But, as God, He can give so much more than that. Remember, although He was fully human, born of Mary, He was at the same time fully God, conceived of the Holy Ghost. He was deity wrapped in humanity. As a human, Christ knows what it is like for us "down here." As God, He can do something about it.

This is why Hebrews 4:15–16 encourages us to bring our needs to His understanding ears: "For we have not an high priest which cannot be touched with the feeling of our infirmities; but was in all points tempted like as we are, yet without sin. Let us therefore come boldly unto the throne of grace, that we may obtain mercy, and find grace to help in time of need."

The gift of Christ's presence means we can confidently bring Him our needs, knowing that He will understand our hearts and impart His grace.

But there's more to this amazing gift.

HE HELPS US

I've been a pastor long enough to know that not everyone approaches Christmas with joy and peace. For many, the merriment of Christmas only serves to mark a heavy underscore beneath their own loss. The empty chair at the table, the missing card from out of state, the tradition that feels so empty without the person who is now gone.

Others struggle under the added financial burdens of the season. A lost job, a fearful setback, a home in foreclosure—and yet Christmas comes whether they are ready for it or not. Parents long to fulfil their children's expectations, but they are staring at an empty bank account.

Scenic Christmas cards and softly glowing lights seem to suggest that this is a season of perfect nostalgia—a time when everyone can rest and reflect in the midst of unified relationships as they make family memories. But reality says otherwise. Real people live lives fraught with loss, pain, and brokenness.

That's why Jesus came.

Consider the first Christmas. Jesus didn't come to a perfect world, and He wasn't born in a perfect setting. He came to a dark world—steeped in sin and riddled with discord and pain. He was born into abject poverty and grew up under the strain of political oppression. Christmas reminds us that this fallen world will never be perfect.

Remember though—this is *God*. He didn't have to come. He didn't have to endure this. And He definitely didn't have to give His life for our sins.

He *chose* to come. He *chose* to leave the splendor of Heaven to dwell amongst the squalor of men. He *chose* to live with us, to know us, to love us. He *chose* to die for us.

And now, He reminds us that He stands ready to help us. Because He is Emmanuel—God with us—we never have to face another need alone. We have God on our side. I love the rhetorical question of Romans 8:31: "What shall we then say to these things? If God be for us, who can be against us?"

So if the very first Christmas meant that God had come to help us, what does this mean for us today, during this Christmas season?

13

It means that we must remember to allow the light of His presence to shine in the darkest of our circumstances. G. Campbell Morgan once said, "What we do in the crisis always depends on whether we see the difficulties in the light of God, or God in the shadow of the difficulties."

Christ's presence wasn't just for Mary and Joseph and the shepherds as they worshiped Him in the manger. It was for us, too. As the eternal God, Christ has promised, "I will never leave thee, nor forsake thee" (Hebrews 13:5). In other words, His presence with us is forever, not just Christmas morning. The next verse spells out the obvious conclusion to this promise: "So that we may boldly say, The Lord is my helper, and I will not fear what man shall do unto me" (Hebrews 13:6).

Psalm 46:1 assures us that God's help is always available: "God is our refuge and strength, **a very present help in trouble.**"

It is said that King George VI was endeared to his country when he and his wife, Queen Elizabeth, refused to leave London during the darkest days of World War II. Although the Germans were relentlessly bombing the city and there was a legitimate fear for the lives of the royal family, the King and Queen stayed with their countrymen. On at least one occasion, they narrowly escaped death when German bombs exploded in a courtyard at Buckingham Palace. Nevertheless, they resolutely stayed and even subjected themselves to the same privations of rationing as the rest of the country.

One London newspaper reported an incident in which the king was inspecting a bombed out section of the city shortly after an air raid. An elderly man recognized his king, and picking his way through the rubble and tangled debris approached him. "You, here," he choked with tear-filled eyes. "You...in the midst of this. You are a good king."

Christmas says the same to us. God choosing to wrap Himself in helpless humanity that He might give Himself for our sins tells us that He is indeed a good King—and a very present help. He came to our darkness, our hopelessness, our ugly sinfulness; and He came to help. And He has promised to never leave us—even in the darkest hours, emptiest ruins, and most tangled events of our lives.

Why is it then—even though we have the gift of His presence—that in the midst of our struggles, our temptations, our griefs, and our burdens, we try to carry on *without God*?

I think we forget that the gift of Christmas is the gift of His presence.

HE CHANGES US

The presence of Christ in our lives is more than a stirring sentiment; it is a radical life change.

From the moment Gabriel announced to Mary that she would carry the Christ child in her womb all the way to the piercing cry of a hungry newborn, Christ's presence changed life for everyone on that first Christmas.

All throughout Christ's ministry, He changed lives. He gave sight to the blind, hearing to the deaf, words to the mute, strength to the lame, healing to the lepers, and even life to the dead. He fed the hungry and comforted the hurting. He taught words of life, and He lived with grace and compassion. He rebuked the proud and forgave the repentant. Everywhere Christ went, He brought change— not always change in circumstances but change in lives.

Then He did the ultimate—He gave His life, bearing in His body the sins of all mankind. And when He rose from the dead three days later, He proved that He has the power to change lives to the fullest extent. When we trust Him as our Saviour, receiving His gift of eternal life (see page 119), He changes us—from the inside out.

Second Corinthians 5:17 says it beautifully: "Therefore if any man be in Christ, he is a new creature: old things are passed away; behold, all things are become new."

As a pastor, I have the opportunity to view this life change over and over again as I watch people trust Christ as their Saviour. I'll never forget the Christmas card one little girl wrote me years ago.

Dear Pastor,

Thank you for this church and for your preaching.
I know that you work very hard to do that stuff. We
are very happy to have you here. This year my dad
learned not to drink and smoke and how to be nice.
Thank you, and God bless you.

Love,
Anna

What little Anna was describing in her dad was the
change that Christ had brought into his life since he had
been saved.

But the change Christ's presence brings doesn't
end at salvation. In fact, I have the opportunity to daily
experience His changing presence in my own life. From
the moment we trust Christ as our Saviour, His presence
can begin to change us. He can change our fear to courage,
our worry to trust, our pride to humility, our selfishness
to love, our bitterness to forgiveness, and our despair
to hope.

These changes don't happen in an instant. That's why I still need to rely on His presence daily. As I walk with Him and grow in Him, He changes me. I'm so thankful for His presence in my life!

Indeed, Christmas *is* a gift! The mighty God came to us. And even today, He offers us the gift of His presence.

The first people to be invited into the presence of Christ in the manger were the shepherds, and they went on their way rejoicing (Luke 2:20). Why? They had been in the very presence of God.

Take time to enjoy His presence this Christmas. Yes, decorate the house, and make cookies with your children. Organize parties, and gather for family celebrations. Bake, shop, wrap, sing, and enjoy. But in the midst of it all, don't forget the incredible gift of His presence.

Even as you fall into the hustle of preparations and the bustle of celebrations, take your burdens, fears, and needs to Christ. Remember He is Emmanuel—God with us. He understands your needs. He even understands *you*. And He is a very present help.

One author pointed out that "Christmas is not about presents, but His presence!" I would add to that statement that Christ's presence actually *is* a present. It is the reason that Christmas is a gift!

CHAPTER TWO

Fear Not
GOD'S MESSAGE OF PEACE

You would think that the season in which we celebrate "peace on earth and good will toward men" would be one of the most relaxed and joyous times of the year. But reality suggests otherwise.

In our stress-infused holiday season, Christmas has become a time of inflamed emotions as people wrestle with driven schedules and personal needs. The sheer financial demands of Christmas drive people to distraction. In November of 2010, *USA Today* reported that money is the number one stressor for American adults. Yet in that same year, it was estimated that consumers would spend about $465 billion during the Christmas season.

Pressure, hurry, and anxiety bend our reactions more towards irritability than "good will toward men." As for "peace on earth," the holiday season accounts for the highest suicide rates of the year. We adorn our houses and streets with merrily twinkling electric lights, but inwardly we're experiencing the darkness of personal loneliness and failed expectations.

Could it be we have failed to unwrap God's gift of peace?

We usually think of peace as the resulting emotion of blessings and good times. When our Christmas purchases are complete and we still have money in the bank, everyone in the family is happy with each other, and our lives have only enough tension to make them interesting—this is the formula for peace, right?

Well, those who first experienced Christmas peace might say otherwise because they had just encountered the most shocking moments of their lives. They needed peace—not to help them enjoy overflowing blessings—but to give them the ability to merely remain stable through difficult circumstances.

Three times throughout the Christmas story, an angel had reason to tell trembling humans, "Fear not." Ironically, even as the very Prince of Peace entered the world, the natural response of those who heard of His arrival was fear.

God's gift of peace is not just for the most serene moments of our lives. It is for the times when negative circumstances spiral out of our control and our emotions churn with fear. It is for the times when inner turmoil seems to suggest that peace is a far-fetched ideal, inaccessible to every day living. This is precisely when we need God's gift of peace.

So, how can we unwrap this Christmas gift?

WE FIND PEACE WHEN WE SURRENDER TO HIS SOVEREIGNTY

The first recipient of the "fear not" message in relation to Jesus' birth was Mary. Luke 1:26–31 records her moment of fear:

And in the sixth month the angel Gabriel was sent from God unto a city of Galilee, named Nazareth, To a virgin espoused to a man whose name was Joseph, of the house of David; and the virgin's name was Mary. And the angel came in unto her, and said, Hail, thou that art highly favoured, the Lord is with thee: blessed art thou among women. And when she saw him, she was troubled at his saying, and cast in her mind what manner of salutation this should be. And the angel said unto her, Fear not, Mary: for thou hast found favour with God. And, behold, thou shalt conceive in thy womb, and bring forth a son, and shalt call his name JESUS.

When Mary initially saw the angel Gabriel, she feared. The Bible says she "cast in her mind what manner of salutation this should be" (Luke 1:29).

Mary's world had just been shaken—on several levels. On the level of basic reasoning, she had no idea how it was possible that she could conceive a child "seeing I know not a man." However, there were greater implications embedded in this announcement. Although we, with the perspective of scriptural hindsight, think primarily of Mary's privilege to be the mother of Christ, she would have had reason to fear great misunderstanding on the part of her family and friends. After all, she wasn't married, and very soon she would have to announce that she was with child. Most wouldn't believe her account of the angel's visit and her claim to moral purity.

No wonder Mary "cast in her mind." This was a lot for anyone to process.

I'll never forget Christmas 2009. Although I had preached Luke 1 messages about Mary and Jesus for many years, that year everything changed. I now personally related Mary's fear and the angel's message to my own life from a new and, frankly, challenging perspective.

The Saturday before Thanksgiving, I received a staggering call from my oldest son, Larry. Unbeknownst to us, Larry had gone in about a month before and presented himself to the doctor for what seemed to Larry a slight health concern. The doctor assumed all was well but ordered an ultrasound and promised that if anything appeared to be wrong, he would call.

Somehow, the doctor forgot to call...for a month. But that morning—the Saturday before Thanksgiving—the doctor did call Larry. Now Larry was telling me on the phone, "I found out today that I need to go in right now for emergency surgery. Dad, I have cancer."

If you've ever heard the word *cancer* in the same sentence as the name of someone you love, you know the mammoth fear that grips your heart with that short, two-syllable word.

Larry's call stunned me. And it filled my mind with questions: How far had the cancer spread? Would today's surgery eliminate it? What other treatments might Larry have to go through? What was his prognosis? Was this terminal? What about Larry's wife, Ashley? This would obviously be an excruciatingly heavy burden for her. They had been married for only a little over two years.

Just a few hours later, Terrie and I met Larry and Ashley at the hospital where Larry underwent a two-hour surgery.

Because this occurred just before the Thanksgiving holiday, various medical staff vacations mandated that we wait several days to receive test results. We were especially concerned because that surgery had already been delayed a month longer than it should have been. We wanted to hear reports from the pathology tests so we would know specifically what kind of cancer this was and how far it had spread, in order to quickly make decisions regarding further treatment. But no one from our large HMO returned our calls. We were beginning to feel lost in the system.

Finally, at the beginning of December, results came trickling in, and Larry went back for more doctor's appointments and further tests. The doctors recommended that Larry schedule another very serious surgery at the end of December. In surgery, the doctor would make a long incision in Larry's stomach, pull out his intestines, and remove the lymphatic tissue in his back before putting everything back in place and stapling the incision closed. After that, Larry would begin chemotherapy.

Needless to say, I read the Christmas story a little differently that year. As we waited and prayed for Larry, I continued to prepare Christmas sermons. But that year, I began to understand the fear that Mary experienced in a way I never had before, and I began to understand the significance of her response.

Of course, it doesn't take the word *cancer* to bring us to fear. Often all it takes is a change of any kind. Perhaps you're there right now—in the grip of fear. Our natural response to the unknown is to "cast in our mind"— deliberating, questioning, evaluating.

Mary, however, moved to another response.

As Mary pondered her situation, the angel spoke two words of assurance: "Fear not." Gabriel had the heavenly perspective—God's perspective. Because of that, he reminded Mary, "For with God nothing shall be impossible" (Luke 1:37).

With that reminder, Mary said the words that many of us have often spoken but have sometimes found difficult to live out, "Be it unto me according to thy word." Mary settled her mind in peace by surrendering to God's sovereignty.

A mental assent to the theological truth of God's sovereignty and a personal choice of trust are vastly

different. The first is a good starting place. The second is where we find peace.

Of course, we have an advantage that Mary didn't have. We have a complete Bible full of the very promises of God. Although I don't fully understand the intricacies of God's sovereignty and man's free will or why God in His perfect goodness allows suffering, I do have some clear black and white promises on which I can hang my questions. When I choose to trust these promises, regardless of my feelings, they bring hope and comfort.

> *Fear thou not; for I am with thee: be not dismayed; for I am thy God: I will strengthen thee; yea, I will help thee; yea, I will uphold thee with the right hand of my righteousness.*—ISAIAH 41:10

> *For I know the thoughts that I think toward you, saith the LORD, thoughts of peace, and not of evil, to give you an expected end.*—JEREMIAH 29:11

> *For I reckon that the sufferings of this present time are not worthy to be compared with the glory which shall be revealed in us.*—ROMANS 8:18

And we know that all things work together for good to them that love God, to them who are the called according to his purpose.—ROMANS 8:28

For our light affliction, which is but for a moment, worketh for us a far more exceeding and eternal weight of glory; While we look not at the things which are seen, but at the things which are not seen: for the things which are seen are temporal; but the things which are not seen are eternal.—2 CORINTHIANS 4:17–18

These promises—and hundreds of others—remind me that I can safely settle my soul on the sovereignty of God. They help me refocus my circumstances on an eternal perspective.

Mary didn't have all the promises of the New Testament. But she did have Gabriel's statement: "For with God nothing shall be impossible" (Luke 1:37). Resisting her natural inclinations to rely on her feelings, she chose to believe that promise and to submit her will to God's sovereignty. In that choice, Mary found peace.

Through Mary, we learn that God is honored when we simply trust Him with the humanly unexplainable and unanswerable. When we make that choice, we find that "the peace of God, which passeth all understanding, shall keep your hearts and minds through Christ Jesus" (Philippians 4:7).

WE FIND PEACE WHEN WE OBEY HIS DIRECTIVES

If Mary had questions about the virgin birth, Joseph had even more! We don't often think about Joseph. To be sure, we include him in the Christmas pageant. He's dressed in a sheet and bathrobe similar to the shepherds, likely distinguished only by a variant costume color. But he doesn't really do anything except just stand there.

One little boy whose teacher asked him to draw a picture of Christmas didn't even get Joseph's name right. He drew a very large man in work clothes, which surprised the teacher.

"Who's that?" the teacher questioned.

"Oh, that's Round John Virgin," came the matter-of-fact reply. Apparently, our carol "Silent Night" doesn't say enough about Mary's husband, so this little boy ascertained for himself the male figure of the beloved Christmas carol.

Despite our omitting Jesus' earthly stepfather from the script, Christmas for young Joseph was very real, and it brought a frighteningly momentous decision. You'll remember that Luke 1:27 records that Mary was "espoused to a man whose name was Joseph."

Jewish espousal, or betrothal, was stronger even than our custom of engagement. By the standards of betrothal, Mary and Joseph were legally married but would wait about a year from their betrothal commitment to consummate the marriage. This meant that nothing but unfaithfulness could end this relationship, and ending it was actually considered divorce.

Mary's announcement that she was with child put Joseph in a real dilemma. He *knew* that he was not the father of the baby Mary was carrying in her womb, and he had no precedent of a virgin birth to make Mary's explanation seem plausible. The only reasonable conclusion was that Mary had been disloyal to him.

Unless he was to risk his marriage on what appeared by all natural explanations to be an unfaithful spouse, he only had two other options—and neither was pleasant. He could have Mary put to death—by stoning—for unfaithfulness. Or he could divorce her.

Interestingly, just as Scripture carefully emphasizes Mary's purity, it also specifically points to Joseph's character. Matthew 1:19 records, "Then Joseph her husband, **being a just man**, and not willing to make her a publick example, was minded to put her away privily." Obviously, Joseph loved Mary, and he didn't want her to suffer. Considering his limited options, he leaned toward a private divorce.

What a heartbreaking—and fearful—decision Joseph faced!

I can imagine the fitful night Joseph endured after Mary told him her news. No doubt, he tossed and turned, weighing his decision from every angle. But no matter which way he looked at it, there were no good answers.

It was in this crisis moment that an angel was once again sent to bring God's message of peace.

> *But while he thought on these things, behold, the angel of the Lord appeared unto him in a dream, saying, Joseph, thou son of David, fear not to take unto thee Mary thy wife: for that which is conceived in her is of the Holy Ghost. And she shall bring forth a son, and thou shalt call his name JESUS: for he shall save his people from their sins.*—MATTHEW 1:20–21

For all of Joseph's reasoning, only God knew the answer. Not only did the angel vouch for Mary's purity, but he explained to Joseph that Mary's son was the promised Saviour. And the angel gave Joseph a simple directive: "Take unto thee Mary thy wife."

For Joseph, the true test of faith would come as he obeyed this simple—but profoundly significant—command. To obey would require great courage.

Believing Mary and becoming her husband would make Joseph one with Mary in her public scorn and ostracism.

Thankfully, however, Joseph chose to unwrap God's gift of peace by following through on God's command. "Then Joseph being raised from sleep did as the angel of the Lord had bidden him, and took unto him his wife: And knew her not till she had brought forth her firstborn son: and he called his name JESUS" (Matthew 1:24–25).

Today, God's Word is not delivered by angels. It is bound between the covers of the completed Bible, and it is taught to us through the indwelling Holy Spirit. When we are faced with a confusing and unsettling decision, we must seek God's answers through the pages of His Word.

Sometimes we find ourselves confused simply because we haven't even allowed God's Word to weigh in on our decision. Like Joseph, we exert great energy into sorting out our options, but we can only do so with a limited set of facts.

God alone knows all the intricacies of each fact involved in any situation. From that vantage point, He instructs us, "Trust in the LORD with all thine heart; and lean not unto thine own understanding" (Proverbs 3:5).

As we choose to obey God's directives, even when they contradict our own understanding, we have the luxury of leaving the results to God. After all, when we fully obey Him, He assumes full responsibility for the outcomes. Thus, in obedience lies peace.

Mary unwrapped God's peace by submitting to His sovereignty. Joseph unwrapped it by obeying God's command. But there is yet another means through which we unwrap this precious gift from God. On the very night of the first Christmas, once again, an angel was sent to declare God's message of peace.

WE FIND PEACE WHEN WE SEEK GOD

In one Christmastime survey, nearly a third of those questioned said that of all the people mentioned in the Christmas story, they identified most with the shepherds.

The shepherds were like us—average, ordinary, working people. Their days were filled with established routines, and they had no reason to suspect they would be singled out for an invitation to the birthplace of the Son of God.

But their mundane lives were completely transformed during one nighttime watch on the hillside: "And there were in the same country shepherds abiding in the field, keeping watch over their flock by night. And, lo, the angel of the Lord came upon them, and the glory of the Lord shone round about them: and they were sore afraid" (Luke 2:8–9).

Like Mary and Joseph before them, the shepherds' response to the angelic Christmas tidings was one of fear. Can you picture these rugged men—hardened by work and weather, yet faithfully tender toward their flocks— stricken and trembling in fear? Where a moment ago they were sharing campfire stories to keep each other awake, they quickly became mute in a fear-induced silence.

A shepherd, no doubt, regularly faced circumstances that would cause most of us to cower in fear. After all, it was their job to defend the sheep. Collectively, this rugged band must have warded off hundreds of predators to protect the sheep. And, as they had grown up in this profession, slaying savage beasts was just part of a day's labor.

But suddenly, on that first Christmas night, this humble company experienced an event for which no one could have prepared them. In a single moment, their confidence was seized by fear, and they fell to the earth trembling.

How do you find peace when you enter the grip of the unexpected?

The angels gave the shepherds the answer to this very question:

And the angel said unto them, Fear not: for, behold, I bring you good tidings of great joy, which shall be to all people. For unto you is born this day in the city of David a Saviour, which is Christ the Lord. And this shall be a sign unto you; Ye shall find the babe wrapped in swaddling clothes, lying in a manger. And suddenly there was with the angel a multitude of the heavenly host praising God, and saying, Glory to God in the highest, and on earth peace, good will toward men.—LUKE 2:10–14

I wish I could have been there to hear the angels deliver these tidings of joy. Thankfully, their message reaches through the millennia to encompass "all people." It is a message of peace for you and me, just as much as it was for the shepherds.

Terrie and I have two sons and two daughters. One summer, when all of our children were young, the boys decided to turn their room into their clubhouse—complete with a "No Girls Aloud" sign on the door. When I pointed out the misspelling to them, they defended themselves by insisting, "But, Dad, girls *are* loud! If they're not allowed, they won't be loud here."

God's message of peace, sent by the angels to shepherds on a lonely Bethlehem hillside, has no such tag of rejection. It knows no boundaries. Race, nationality, social status, gender—none of these are barriers to God's peace.

Now we can face the unexpected with the gift of peace. But we must listen carefully to the joyous message delivered by the heavenly host, as they proclaimed the basis for this peace: "Unto you is born…a Saviour, which is Christ the Lord."

Jesus Himself is the peace-giver. When we know Him as Saviour, we know the peace of sins forgiven. When we know Him as Lord, we know the peace of His authority in our lives. Hence, we come to know peace by knowing the Prince of Peace Himself!

This angelically heralded message literally transformed the shepherds. As the message of peace penetrated their hearts, they looked at each other in wonder and excitement. "And it came to pass, as the angels were gone away from them into heaven, the shepherds said one to another, Let us now go even unto Bethlehem, and see this thing which is come to pass, which the Lord hath made known unto us. And they came with haste, and found Mary, and Joseph, and the babe lying in a manger" (Luke 2:15–16).

How did they respond to the message of peace? They beat a path to the manger! And when they got there, they found themselves in the presence of God Himself!

We try so hard to manufacture our own peace, to surround ourselves with an impenetrable bubble of security. We put our confidence in our families, jobs, friends, health, intelligence, and any number of other assets. But in our most vulnerable moments, we recognize that all of these can disappear in a heartbeat.

When the unexpected comes and our bubble is popped, what happens then?

Our ultimate confidence must be in God. But we can only experience the security of His presence as we, like the shepherds, make an effort to seek Him.

Do you know the presence of Christ in your life? Jeremiah 29:13 promises, "And ye shall seek me, and find me, when ye shall search for me with all your heart." God encourages us to "draw near with a true heart in full assurance of faith" (Hebrews 10:22). Through Christmas, Christ gave us the gift of His presence. He is Emmanuel—

God with us. But we only find peace in His presence as we choose to seek Him.

Although we have no tangible manger to visit, His written Word is as near as our fingertips. Through its promises, God comforts us. Through its commands, He guides us. Through its words, He lovingly whispers, "Fear not—I am with you."

It is tragic that the very season we celebrate Christ's birth is so busy that we hardly have time to really seek God—to shut out the world and seek His face through the pages of Scripture.

The shepherds recognized the incredible privilege of being invited into the presence of Christ. They forgot their livelihood and rushed to gaze into the tiny face in the manger. We must follow the footsteps of these men. We too must demonstrate a desire to be near our Saviour. It will never happen—not consistently anyway—unless we are willing to make it a priority.

And what a transformation the presence of God can make in a life! When we first met the shepherds, they were on a starlit hillside, trembling in fear over the unexpected visit from the heavenly messengers. But our last glimpse of these same shepherds is in Luke 2:17 as they joyfully share the news of Christmas with all who will listen.

What made the difference? In their moment of fear, they heard God's message of peace. And they unwrapped this gift by entering the presence of God.

I'm thankful that Scripture is transparent about the fears of Mary, Joseph, and the shepherds. Most of us keep these things to ourselves. But as God allowed us a glimpse into these trembling souls in their most vulnerable moments, He gave us an example of how to unwrap His gift of peace.

Are you facing an overwhelming situation? Acknowledge your fear to God and then submit to His sovereignty. Claim His promises and trust His purposes.

Are you in the throws of a confusing decision? Listen for God's counsel and obey His directives.

Are you reeling from an unexpected shock? Seek God's presence with diligent faith.

When fear reaches in to grip our hearts, God has a gentle message of peace: *fear not*. This is the gift of Christmas.

CHAPTER THREE

Unusual Packages
A FRESH LOOK AT GOD'S SURPRISES

I'll never forget the look on my ten-year-old son Matt's face when he received his Christmas gift as a special delivery from the mailman.

For months, Matt had been pestering Terrie and me to get him a puppy. We already had a family dog, but Matt was sure that he needed his very own dog. Of course he promised he would care for it diligently and love it dearly. Matt was so adamant that there was no room to question his sincerity, but Terrie and I were skeptical of his commitment.

Nevertheless, when the doorbell rang on Christmas Eve, we sent Matt to answer the door. Who should be standing there but a postal carrier (a kind mailman in our church who agreed to wear his postal uniform to help us deliver this gift) with a large—and wiggly—box addressed to "Matthew Chappell."

Matt was delighted! He promptly named his puppy Krispy, and for several days, the two were inseparable. (After that, Terrie and I were correct in our mistrust of Matt's commitment!) But regardless of the fact that we soon found ourselves caring for two family dogs, it was fun to see Matthew receive his special and unusually delivered package.

Another Christmas, I wanted to give Terrie a piece of nice jewelry, but I didn't want her to guess what it was before she opened it. So I wrapped up the jewelry box in beautiful wrapping paper. I then placed the wrapped jewelry box in a slightly larger box and wrapped that box. And then another box….Before I was done, the jewelry was encased in five wrapped boxes. And I loved watching Terrie open every one of them!

It's fun to receive a gift in an unusual package—especially if the packaging helps build anticipation and then reveals a desired possession. But what if the unusual package is an *unwanted* package?

I once read a list of nine common responses to unusual Christmas gifts. Perhaps you've stammered out a few of these:

9. "Well, well, well, now, *there's* a gift!"

8. "With all the hostile takeovers this year, I missed the big Ronco/K-Tel/Ginsu merger. Would you just look at that! What will they think of next?!"

7. "NO, really, I didn't know that there was a Chia Pet tie! OH, wow! It's a clip-on too!"

6. "You know, I always wanted one of these! Jog my memory—what's it called again?"

5. "You know what? I'm going to find a very special place to put this!"

4. "Boy, you don't see craftsmanship like *that* every day!"

3. "And it's such an interesting color, too!"

2. "You say that was the last one? Am I sure glad that you snapped that baby up!"

And…the number one thing to say about the gift you didn't want:

1. "You shouldn't have! No, really, I mean it, you really shouldn't have!"

Life has a way of handing us unexpected and unwanted packages. A pink slip from your employer. A bad report from the doctor. An eviction notice from the bank. A harsh email from a strained relationship. Papers served by your spouse—or a divorce announced by your parents. Too often, the package delivered with your name on it isn't a present you want.

The first Christmas was wrapped in an unusual set of circumstances. And it reveals to us that the "surprises" in our lives that look so foreboding truly are an unusual packaging of God's grace. Through the account of the first Christmas, we learn how to unwrap bulky, heavy packages that we would have never chosen for ourselves.

What can you do when life hands you an unwanted package?

_____

RECOGNIZE THAT UNUSUAL PACKAGES ARE FILTERED THROUGH THE PROVIDENCE OF GOD

I can imagine Mary and Joseph's dismay when they first heard the "decree from Caesar Augustus, that all the world should be taxed" (Luke 2:1). And it wasn't just the tax that would have bothered them. In fact, the tax was the least of their worries.

This particular tax order was a double directive—a census as well as a taxation. To best account for each individual, the government required these people to go to the city of their lineage for the proceedings. Unfortunately, the timing of the census was precisely the same timing as Mary's due date.

The decree was issued by Caesar Augustus who ruled from 27 BC to 14 AD. He was the first emperor of the Roman Empire, and he accomplished several notable achievements. He established the first fire fighting and police forces in Rome. He commanded 170,000 soldiers and maintained the Roman roads throughout Italy. Of course, just as today, this progress was expensive—thus the tax.

If you don't mind adding a bit of imagination to the story, picture Mary and Joseph as they listen to the herald coming through Nazareth to proclaim the decree: "Hear, ye; hear ye. All Jewish persons must report to the city of their birth for the emperor's census. This public accounting will take place three months from today. No exceptions."

Can you see Mary and Joseph as they look at each other in concern and then, just to be sure, count off how many weeks Mary has left until the baby will arrive? Yes, it was just as they thought. The census was ordered for the same week as Mary's due date. Well, they would just have to do the best they could! And they could always hope that Jesus would be born early.

But He wasn't born early, and when the time of the census came, Mary and Joseph prepared for the trip. Joseph may have found an extra blanket to cushion Mary's ride (a first-century shock absorber!). And Mary gathered swaddling clothes for this special baby. Together they began the over-seventy-mile journey.

Inconvenient? Yes.

Stressful? No doubt.

Frightening? For sure.

Yet we know today that this trip was woven into the tapestry of God's intricate providence in the birth of His Son.

We are often surprised by the frustrating delivery of unusual packages in our lives, but nothing takes God by surprise. In fact, in the affairs of men, God often orchestrates behind the scenes to conform events outside of our control to His divine plan.

Seven hundred years before Mary and Joseph made their way to Bethlehem, God had instructed the prophet Micah to record, "But thou, Bethlehem Ephratah, though thou be little among the thousands of Judah, yet out of thee shall he come forth unto me that is to be ruler in Israel; whose goings forth have been from of old, from everlasting" (Micah 5:2). Thus, Mary and Joseph's journey to Bethlehem was no accident. It was the fulfillment of a prophecy concerning where Jesus would be born.

The timing of this taxing is fascinating. It was actually decreed in 8 BC corresponding with Luke 2:2 ("And this taxing was first made when Cyrenius was governor of Syria"). But it did not hit Palestine until a couple of years later, around 5 BC (which was actually the year in which Christ was born). This means that even years before Christ was born, God moved the most powerful ruler at the time to require a taxing which would fulfill His prophecy that the Christ child would be born in Bethlehem.

This gives a new perspective to the journey to Bethlehem.

Was it a difficult package to receive? Yes. But it was filtered by God's providence. And Mary and Joseph unwrapped it with grace. Without a word of complaint recorded, they traveled to Bethlehem.

Life is full of unavoidable circumstances. We can expend our energy in futile efforts to change them. We can spend our time stewing in bitter resentment over

them. Or we can trust God's providence in the midst of them.

Of course, we may not see His hand of providence for years to come. I don't know if Mary and Joseph understood the significance of their journey to Bethlehem at the time. But these were just two of the many people in the pages of Scripture who faced unavoidable circumstances and later learned that God's hand of providence had been working through those very difficulties all along.

Joseph (of the Old Testament) was sold into slavery by his own brothers. Yet, from his new location in Egypt, and even *because* of his years in the Egyptian prison, he was promoted to a position from which he was able to save his family from starvation.

David arrived at the forsaken battlefield with food supplies for his soldier brothers. This errand imposed on him by his father actually brought him to the scene of one of the greatest victories in the entire Bible—a victory in which he was able to be the hero.

Daniel was taken captive into Babylon—ripped from his home and family. But it was in Babylon that he saw God close the mouths of hungry lions and received some of the most specific end-time prophecies recorded in the Old Testament.

Esther was required to marry a heathen king. Early in her reign, the second in command under her husband conceived a wicked plan to exterminate Esther's people. Her position in the palace gave her the leverage she needed to turn the tables on Haman's plan.

And then there is *you*. Do you have unpreventable circumstances seeming to thwart your plans? Could they be wrapped in the providence of God—actual gifts to benefit your life?

Anything out of our control is filtered by the hand of our loving Father. Although we know that God does not order or cause sin (James 1:13), we can also rest assured that anything that comes into our lives is directed by His providence. He never allows what He cannot make good in His promise of Romans 8:28, "And we know that **all things** work together for good to them that love God, to them who are the called according to his purpose."

Sometimes, unusual packages are God's most precious gifts. Trust the filter of His loving providence, and you will often see His plan in the end.

ALLOW YOUR RESPONSE TO SHOWCASE GOD'S GRACE

Perhaps the all-time winner for most unusual wrapping of a precious gift was the Bethlehem manger. For here in this crude cradle lay the Creator of the world.

A few years ago, my family and I had the opportunity to tour Israel. This was a trip of a lifetime, and I learned so much just by seeing and experiencing the sites of biblical history.

One artifact, however, was particularly surprising to me as it looked much different than I had always pictured. It was an ancient manger. I've always pictured a wooden manger. In fact, many pictures of the nativity scene— which are probably more westernized and modernized than we realize—depict a gentle hay-lined manger that could almost pass for a rustic crib.

The manger I saw in Israel, however, jolted my preconceived ideas. What I found was a crude stone trough. Hard. Unyielding. Foreboding. How would you like to lay your baby in *that?*

On top of the fact that Jesus' manger was most likely made of stone, consider that it would also have been dirty. If you're not familiar with livestock, pay a visit to a local farmer and ask to look at the troughs from which he feeds the animals. I can assure you, they wouldn't come anywhere near passing a hospital inspection in the United States. Layered underneath with cobwebs and coated inside with slobber-caked dust, it's not the sort of place you would want to lay your newborn baby.

And yet, when Jesus came to us, He actually chose to first lay His head in a manger. The contrast between the crudeness of the manger and the beauty of Christ, the filth of the stable and the purity of the Son of God, is striking. That simple piece of chiseled stone became a showcase for the wondrous grace of God. Its very contrast emphasized Christ's humility and grace.

When our family was in Israel, I remember standing in the cave in Bethlehem where Jesus may have been born. (Caves were sometimes used as stables in the first century.) I read the Christmas story aloud, and we took some time to thank the Lord for His willingness to come to Earth and be born in a manger.

The presentation of Christ to this world was not the way we would have planned it. And I think we can safely say it is not the way Mary would have planned it either! But, with the enabling grace of God, Mary's response to the reception of the unusual package of the manger magnified God's grace, rather than opening it up for question.

Mary could have complained. She could have become angry toward God. "God, first You make me travel over seventy miles when I'm great with child, and now this?! Couldn't I at least have a comfortable room and clean surroundings in which to give birth? Why would You do this to me?"

Joseph, too, could easily have been able to justify some anger. "Lord, I never would have planned it this way—ever. I wanted to make it comfortable for Mary. I wanted to provide for her. And yet, from every angle this pregnancy and birth has been too much for me to handle. That's it; I'm done."

What life does *to* us often depends on what life finds *in* us. Because Mary and Joseph received the incredible gift of Jesus—with no expectations of how He should be delivered or presented to the world—they deflected the attention from themselves to the manger. And before this small showcase of grace, shepherds knelt in worship toward God.

What do you do when life hands you an unwanted package? Allow your response to God's providence to showcase His grace. Receive His gifts without murmuring. After all, that very package may be the encasement of extravagant grace!

BE WHOLLY YIELDED SO HE CAN WORK HIS PURPOSES IN AND THROUGH YOU

Let's go back to the pre-Bethlehem part of the Christmas story and remember why God was willing to give Mary such an unusual package. Why was Mary the recipient of such a special gift, even if it was unusually wrapped? Would it not be reasonable to guess that there were other Jewish girls who would have fit the requirement of purity for being the earthly mother of Christ? Mary definitely wasn't perfect. Scripture never tells us to pray to her, and even she acknowledged that she needed a Saviour (Luke 1:46–47). Yet, Gabriel told her she was "highly favoured" (Luke 1:28). Why did God choose Mary?

The complete answer to that question is known only by God. But it is significant that Mary was willing—truly submitted—to receive this unusual, and in some ways heavy, gift.

Sure, there was great cost involved for Mary. But she yielded to the Lord, bore the cost, and cherished the gift.

Mary actually had what to us might be several strikes against her. She was poor. She was engaged to a poor man. She was not popular or influential. In fact, even her hometown of Nazareth was disdained for its rough citizens and lack of influence.

One writer questioned, "Why Nazareth? Because there God found a woman who was completely yielded to His purpose for her life. Great works of God rarely start in big places. Rather, they start in small places—in some person with a big commitment."

God isn't looking for the strong or searching for the famous. He gives His most precious gifts—albeit unusually wrapped—to those who will simply yield their wills to Him. Our problem is that we see what looks to us like distasteful wrapping, and in our selfishness, we plead with God to take back His gifts.

Not so with Mary. She simply said, "Behold the handmaid of the Lord; be it unto me according to thy word" (Luke 1:38). William Barclay said the world's most popular prayer is, "Thy will be changed." But the greatest prayer is, "Thy will be done." Thankfully, Mary prayed the latter.

What about you? Are you staggering under the load of an unusual package—one that you never would have chosen, but have no way to release? Are you struggling to understand the unavoidable circumstances that have come into your life? Are you disappointed in the harsh realities of failed expectations—crushed dreams that you thought would be played out so differently?

If so, tiptoe to the Bethlehem stable. Gaze on the weary young mother, required to travel far in her last month of pregnancy—only to find a barn in which to give birth. See a crude manger—wiped down, surely, but nonetheless, still dirty. But don't look solely at these wrappings. Peer beyond, into the manger, and see the face of God! Although the presentation of Christ to this world was not the way we would have planned it, it was wrapped in grace and laced with intricate providence.

Yes, Christmas is a gift. And sometimes God sends His greatest gifts in the most unusual packages. Trust His providence. Showcase His grace. And wholly surrender to His will. In time, you will learn that God gives the best surprises.

CHAPTER FOUR

No Room

WHY WE DON'T RECEIVE HIS LOVE

For thousands of ladies around America, Black Friday shopping is a non-negotiable event, ranking right up there on the calendar with Christmas itself. My wife, along with our daughters and daughters-in-law, usually gets in on the occasion. One year, Terrie and the girls even downloaded Black Friday shopping applications to their smartphones. Together they browsed for the most alluring bargains and then devised a plan of attack to rake in the best deals. Each person was assigned a different post (store) for the opening moment—4:00 AM.

Although the ladies in our family aren't quite this dedicated every year, they usually return with loaded shopping bags and hundreds of dollars worth of savings. (Sometimes I question if it is really worth it to spend hundreds in order to save hundreds, but my wife assures me it is. In over thirty years of marriage, I've learned that she's usually right; so I must be missing something here.)

I'm not planning to get in on the Black Friday opportunities anytime soon. For one thing, these day-after-Thanksgiving crowds seem to know little of Thanksgiving generosity or Christmas cheer. I even read of one poor man who made his way to the store long before the early opening. Already, there was a large throng blocking the entrance. The quiet and unassuming man tried to squeeze his way toward the door, but he was pushed back on every attempt and even punched by a few irate women. Three times he repeated his efforts. And three times he was pushed and knocked back.

As he picked himself up from the parking lot after his third try, someone overheard him say, "That does it! If they hit me one more time, I'm not going to open the store!"

Little did these greedy shoppers realize they were refusing entrance to the one they most needed.

And that was, in a far more significant sense, the situation on that first Christmas, a little over two thousand years ago. Christ came to a world that desperately needed Him. But they either didn't recognize who He was, or they didn't care. "He came unto his own, and his own received him not" (John 1:11).

The innkeeper rejected Him.

Herod sought to kill Him.

The rest of the world ignored Him.

While the most significant event since Creation took place, occupants of Bethlehem continued with "business as usual." They either had no room, no time, or no interest for the One they needed most.

And this pattern has continued throughout history, right into our present day. Christmas has become anything but a celebration of Jesus Christ.

Merchants commercialize Christmas, making it the most lucrative (or impoverishing—depending which side of the checkout stand you're on) holiday of the year.

Secularists reject Christmas, insisting on the more politically correct "Happy Holidays" greeting.

As Christians, we are not exempt. We often simply forget the true reason for Christmas.

Unfortunately, it's not just on this one obvious day of the year that we leave no room for Christ—it's not just Christmas. If we're not careful, all year long we will ignore the One we need most. We crowd Him out of our schedules and make no room for Him in our busy lives.

Why do we exclude Christ? Could our reasons be the same as the innkeeper who said there was no room on that first Christmas so many years ago?

WE DON'T REALIZE HOW MUCH WE NEED HIM

To understand the tragedy of making no room for Christ, think back to the first person who said "no room." You know the story: Mary and Joseph made their way to Bethlehem for the census. As they arrived in town, they searched in vain for a place to stay. Unfortunately, there was "no room for them in the inn" (Luke 2:7).

Little did he realize it, but this shrewd, business-minded innkeeper was missing more than an opportunity to show kindness. He was turning away the Saviour of the world.

We too easily think of making room for Christ in our lives as something like "patronizing God" (although we'd never come right out and say it in such a fashion). If we miss church or crowd personal worship out of our schedules, we don't realize what we're missing. We just figure we'll do it next time…if next time is more convenient.

We often fail to recognize the fact that it's not *God* who needs fulfillment by being part of our lives. It's *us*. When we reject or ignore Christ, we are excluding the One who came to give us the love of the Father and the only One who can fill the empty places in our lives with purpose and meaning.

But in our quest for happiness, we crowd our lives with that which is of little or no significance.

Often, materialism is the culprit. Although millions of Americans are feeling the crushing weight of the economic downturn, we are still materialistically minded. Whether we have money or we don't, we believe it will make us happy, and we physically or mentally pursue it. Thus, life becomes a race to accumulate the most.

On a flight, I took a few moments to flip through the airline catalog in my seat. Perhaps it was just my mood at the moment, but the absurdity of what people will actually purchase greatly humored me:

EASTER ISLAND MONOLITH STATUE
Astound and impress guests at your next Polynesian luau with our exclusive, heavyweight, six-foot-tall King Moai, inspired by the 380 AD Easter Island originals.

JOHN WAYNE MONOPOLY
Celebrate the life of one of the most beloved actors of our time. Buy, sell and trade the most significant properties in John Wayne's professional and personal life such as Winterset, IA; Kyoto, Japan; and Monument Valley in your quest to own it all.

MAESTRO MOUSE

Our exclusive, diminutive pianist plays twelve Christmas favorites on his grand piano, from "Jingle Bells" to "Away in a Manger." To begin the concert, place a miniature music sheet onto the holder. Maestro announces the song's title, the tune begins, and the piano keys move up and down to the song.

These items may have value to some people (particularly as good gifts for the person who already has everything!), but as a list, they struck me as particularly clever gimmicks. And they reminded me of just how materialistic Americans have become. While much of the world is struggling in true poverty and real hunger, we are so pampered that we need to start inventing gifts—gifts that earn more points for creativity than practicality!

What is the problem with materialism? It crowds out Christ. Literally, we have no room for Him in our lives. When we become so obsessed with working, hoarding, protecting, and saving that we don't have time to worship Christ or serve others in His name, we miss the significance of life.

The truth is, we *need* Christ.

We need Him more than we need any other possession.

We need Him more than we need any other relationship.

We need Him more than we need any other promotion, recognition, achievement, employment, or *anything*.

We need to make Christ the center of our lives. Not for *His* sake. He's God. We need Him for *our* sakes.

If you could time travel back to first-century Bethlehem and stand on the doorstep of the inn where Mary and Joseph sought lodging, I think you would argue with the innkeeper. "Look, man! Do you know who you're turning away?! You're making the mistake of your life. You could be the one to provide a 'birthing room' for your Saviour!"

It's easy to see the innkeeper's mistake in hindsight. But what about today? Do you recognize your need to make room for Christ in your life? To worship Him? To make Him the center rather than fitting Him in where there's room?

Make room for Him this Christmas. Take time to worship Him. Thank Him for coming for you. Determine that your Christmas—and the rest of your year—will not be about finding ways to advance yourself, but will center around knowing Him.

When you make room for Christ, you will find you have made room to experience and unwrap the love of God. Christ came to bring us the love of the Father, but we are too often quick to reject that which we need most.

Even if we understand our need for Christ, there is another reason we are slow to make room for Him.

WE AREN'T WILLING TO ADJUST OUR LIVES

The emperor's census must have given the innkeeper the financial opportunity of a lifetime. No doubt he filled every room in his inn and even improvised additional corners for those willing to take them. When he told

Mary and Joseph, "Sorry, there's no room here," I'm sure he wasn't bluffing.

But I wonder, where did the innkeeper sleep that night? Perhaps he could have given up *his* room.

Even little Trevor figured this out. He was assigned the role of the innkeeper in the school Christmas pageant. As a tenderhearted seven year old, he struggled to fill this heartless role. With much coaching, however, he learned to fold his arms across his chest and bellow, "No room here! Can't you see I'm filled to capacity. Look somewhere else!"

But by the night of the performance, this boy-turned-innkeeper couldn't take it any longer. As Mary and Joseph dejectedly walked away from his rejection, he forgot his acting and called out after them, "Wait! You can have my room!"

It ruined the play, but it sealed the point.

We can make room for Christ if we really want to.

I don't know anyone who isn't legitimately busy. In fact, most of us are running at a frantic pace, trying to keep up with a task list that seems to multiply exponentially every day. But think about it: all of us make room for what is important to us. We just need to be willing to adjust our lives.

I heard about a frazzled mother who represents far too many of us at Christmas time. She was shopping with her three-year-old son on Christmas Eve. As you can imagine, she had a long list of gifts to purchase and a short amount of time. As she rushed from store to store, she struggled to keep her little one with her. At one store, she realized she had lost track of her son and retraced her steps to find him.

Little Johnny was standing outside with his nose pressed flat against the frosty window. "Johnny, we need to hurry," she chided as she rushed to his side.

"Look, Mommy! It's Jesus!" he responded, his eyes reverently riveted on a nativity scene displayed through the window. "Baby Jesus is there in the hay!"

"Johnny!" his mother said with exasperation. "We don't have time for that. Can't you see that Mommy is trying to get ready for Christmas?!" She pried Johnny away from the window and hurried back into the store, unaware that it was Johnny who was truly celebrating Christmas.

In our rush to fill our lives, we often miss what life is all about. Without even giving it a second thought, we say, "Sorry, Jesus. No room here."

Take the challenge to make room for worship this Christmas. Recognize how immensely you need Christ. It will make you willing to readjust your schedule to worship Him and thank Him for the gift of His love.

Although the only Christmas in which Christ was physically born is past, He has given us *today*—our opportunity to make room for Him. But there is another reason we often miss the opportunity—it's the most obvious reason that the innkeeper turned Mary and Joseph away on the first Christmas.

WE DON'T REALIZE WHO HE IS

The story is told of a struggling community who called an open town meeting to discuss their financial straits.

Included in the group of a couple dozen people at the meeting was a stranger. No one knew him, and no one paid him any attention. In fact, once when he tried to speak up, he was interrupted as the townspeople continued to hash out possible solutions. Soon the stranger left.

A few minutes after he left, a late-arriving town resident ran breathlessly into the meeting. "What was *he* doing here?" he asked excitedly. "Is he going to help us?"

"Who?" the others looked at the man with surprise. "You mean that stranger? Who was he anyway?"

"You mean you really don't know?" The latecomer's body sagged with disappointment. "That was John D. Rockefeller. His yacht is in our harbor. Didn't you get his help?"

This town missed its golden opportunity because they didn't know who Rockefeller was.

Does this story sound familiar? I wonder if the innkeeper of Bethlehem ever realized who *he* had turned away. Mary and Joseph surely didn't come to him saying, "We're going to have a baby, and you need to know that this child is the Son of God. If you don't make room for us here, you will regret it for the rest of your life." No, they just made their need known and left when the innkeeper had no room.

Although we will never stand in the innkeeper's position, with the opportunity to provide the birthing room for Christ, we are daily surrounded with countless opportunities to give to Christ. Usually, however, we're slow to recognize them for what they are.

But Matthew 25:34–40 records that the Lord Himself pays careful attention to these opportunities, and when He returns as King, He will reward those who recognize them:

> Then shall the King say unto them on his right hand, Come, ye blessed of my Father, inherit the kingdom prepared for you from the foundation of the world: For I was an hungred, and ye gave me meat: I was thirsty, and ye gave me drink: I was a stranger, and ye took me in: Naked, and ye clothed me: I was sick, and ye visited me: I was in prison, and ye came unto me. Then shall the righteous answer him, saying, Lord, when saw we thee an hungred, and fed thee?

or thirsty, and gave thee drink? When saw we thee a stranger, and took thee in? or naked, and clothed thee? Or when saw we thee sick, or in prison, and came unto thee? And the King shall answer and say unto them, Verily I say unto you, Inasmuch as ye have done it unto one of the least of these my brethren, ye have done it unto me.

Did you catch it? Christ has so identified Himself with the needy—especially needy Christians—that He says we are caring for *Him* when we reach out to *them*. If we have no room in our lives to serve others in the name of Christ, we choose to miss the greatest opportunities of life.

James 1:27 emphasizes this point: "Pure religion and undefiled before God and the Father is this, To visit the fatherless and widows in their affliction, and to keep himself unspotted from the world."

In our church, we've emphasized ministries through which we can give the compassionate love of Christ to others: missions (giving financially so those around the world who have never heard of Christ may know

Him), visiting our own widows and caring for their needs, ministering in rest homes around town, and many other ministries.

Through the years, our bus ministry has consistently reached out and given to others. Every week, members of our church give of their time to visit children in our community—many of which are from underprivileged neighborhoods and broken homes—and bring these children to church on a bus.

A few months ago, our ministry received an email about one of our former bus riders that reminded me afresh of the importance of making room in our lives for loving others in Jesus' name.

> I am an English instructor at Roosevelt High School in Los Angeles. This past week, I assigned the writing of a speech celebrating Valentine's Day. One student, named Kevin, wrote a remarkable essay about your church.
>
> Kevin spoke of a "bus captain" named Brother Andrew....I have paraphrased the speech below. It stirred my heart, as a Christian, and caused several students to speak with Kevin about his faith.

Today I want to speak to everyone on what I think is true love. Love is not a movie or a feeling or an emotion. Love is God. I used to live in Palmdale with my family. There was a church there called Lancaster Baptist. The church sent buses out to pick up people in our apartment complex and take us to their church.

Brother Andrew was my bus captain. Andrew was my friend; he showed me for the first time what it felt like to be really loved. My parents left my family when I was eleven, so we lived with my uncle there in Palmdale. Andrew told me that I still needed to love and talk to God about my parents, even though they had hurt me.

Andrew always told me that he loved me, but he could never love me anywhere close to as much as God did. God loved me so much that he came to earth as a human named Jesus. Jesus died for all of us. How many of your boyfriends or girlfriends would really do that for you? Is that really love? No, it is not. Love is what I saw on that bus....

Andrew would come to our apartment two or three times a week just to talk or hang out. He would come and talk to my uncle about Jesus and they would talk for hours about how to stop drinking and messing around with girls. Andrew would come get us after school, and we would go to the park or grab some food.

Andrew had no responsibility or reason to do any of this. He told me of a church and a pastor named Pastor Chappell that loved me. They would give of their money to run the buses. That is true love. Why would they love us kids like that? Because they wanted to tell us of a much bigger love, the love of God....

There are other "Kevins" in the world. Many of them probably cross your path on a regular basis. Of course, they don't come to you and say, "Hi, I'm Kevin, and I really need love. If you will help me, you will be helping Jesus." And so, like the innkeeper of Bethlehem, we usually don't recognize those who need help for who they are.

But when we give of ourselves to share the love of Christ with others, we not only minister to their needs, but we also experience the joy of Christmas. Giving Christ's love is the best way to unwrap this priceless gift.

Don't fall into the Christmas trap of "too busy." Those two words are just a rephrasing of the innkeeper's line, "no room." Christ didn't come to Bethlehem because *He* needed it. He came for us. And when you worship Christ this Christmas and give to others in His name, it will be *you* who benefits most.

Make room for the gift of Christmas. It is the opportunity of a lifetime.

CHAPTER FIVE

Songs in the Night
EXPRESSING THE JOY OF CHRISTMAS

Three-year-old Tyler and his older sister, Allison, were singing Christmas carols in the back seat of the car while their mother drove from store to store. As Tyler concluded "Silent Night," he finished with the words, "Sleep in heavenly beans."

"No, silly," five-year-old Allison corrected him. "It's not *beans*; it's *peas*."

The truth is, whatever you might sleep in—beans, peas, a bed, or even a manger—if you know Christ, you can rest in His peace and rejoice in His love. In fact, if there is anything the Christmas story emphasizes, it is that Christ's presence brings songs—even in the night.

As a little boy, I knew that nighttime (a.k.a. bedtime) was an unpleasant experience. I took my time brushing my teeth and getting into my pajamas before that final moment came when I had to resign myself to ending the day under my quilt.

Years ago, I overcame my dislike for bed. (Having children has a way of doing that for you!) Now, I look forward to it. But there is still a form of night that I dread. It's not the physical night when the sun goes down, but a variant form of night, when heavy burdens settle and a night season of the soul sets in.

Christmas reminds us, however, that God bestows some of His most lavish gifts in the night seasons. Jesus Himself was probably born sometime between dusk and dawn. And His birth gives us every reason to experience the joy of Christmas all year round—day or night.

———

CHRISTMAS NIGHT

Have you ever noticed how many of our Christmas carols remind us that the first Christmas songs were sung in the night?

Silent Night
O Holy Night
It Came Upon a Midnight Clear
Away in a Manger
O Little Town of Bethlehem
While Shepherds Watched Their Flocks

The Light of the World came to earth in the dark of night. While Bethlehem slept and shepherds watched their flocks, Mary gave birth to the One who came to bring us light and joy.

Perhaps you are experiencing a dark night season. Relationships have caved in. Medical test results have come back with frightening news. Circumstances out of your control are closing in on you. Where you once basked in the light of day, you now perceive simply black nothingness.

Night is no respecter of Christmas. Even during this most joyous time of the year, darkness can descend upon us.

On the other hand, Christmas is no respecter of night. In fact, Christmas is all about joy in the night! Christ Himself came in the night, and He is the God who gives us "songs in the night" (Job 35:10).

From the first praises of a young Jewish girl to the jubilant songs of angels and the glad shouts of shepherds, we find that Christmas is a time to sing in the night.

What do we sing about in the night?

WE REJOICE IN GOD'S FAITHFULNESS

The first "Christmas carol" was sung months before Christ's birth. And it was composed by the first human being to know of His arrival.

And Mary said, My soul doth magnify the Lord, And my spirit hath rejoiced in God my Saviour. For he hath regarded the low estate of his handmaiden: for, behold, from henceforth all generations shall call me blessed. For he that is mighty hath done to me great things; and holy is his name. And his mercy is on them that fear him from generation to generation. He hath shewed strength with his arm; he hath scattered the proud in the imagination of their hearts. He hath put down the mighty from their seats, and exalted them of low degree. He hath filled the hungry with good things; and the rich he hath sent empty away. He hath holpen his servant Israel, in remembrance of his mercy; As he spake to our fathers, to Abraham, and to his seed for ever.—LUKE 1:46–55

Perhaps the most touching aspect of this song of praise is its spontaneity. Mary was not singing words memorized from a childhood hymnal. She was not mechanically repeating phrases by rote with no insight to their meaning. Her song was the overflow of a heart rejoicing in a faithful God. These words sprang forth from the depths of her soul.

But notice the content of Mary's spontaneous song. Her praise was an echo of Hannah's praise in 1 Samuel 2:1–10. The two songs are so parallel that many have noticed their similarities. This young woman, the mother of the Lord Jesus Christ, knew Scripture so well that it freely flowed from her lips.

Colossians 3:16 instructs all of us, "Let the word of Christ dwell in you richly in all wisdom; teaching and admonishing one another in psalms and hymns and spiritual songs, singing with grace in your hearts to the Lord." When we make God's Word the center of our thinking, we too will sing spiritual songs of joy and praise.

How is this relevant to us today? Our culture tells us that joy is found in favorable circumstances. Deeply ingrained into our thinking is the belief that we can be happy when life goes well. A raise at work, a good score on a test at school, an unexpected word of praise, attaining our desired weight or accomplishing our list of goals—all of these define our happiness, right?

Achievement, encouragement, and success are wonderful gifts from God, and we should thank Him for them. But none of these, singularly or in combination, provide a solid foundation for lasting joy.

What happens when they are gone? What if life is *not* going well? What if we lose our job, fail the test, disappoint those we love, and miss every one of the goals we charted for ourselves?

Christmas teaches us that true joy is not the absence of trouble; it is the presence of Christ.

Consider Mary. Shortly before her song of praise, she learned she was about to experience a great deal of misunderstanding. In fact, in some ways, the presence of Christ in Mary's life actually created some troubles. Even Simeon prophesied to Mary, "a sword shall pierce through thy own soul" (Luke 2:35). From Jesus' birth until Mary watched His crucifixion, she knew a depth of grief that dispelled any notion in her mind that joy is rooted in a painless life.

Actually, it was because Mary's joy was *not* based in her circumstances that she was able to praise God for His presence in the midst of her circumstances. And it was through the Old Testament Scriptures that Mary understood the wondrous significance of the presence of God in her life.

Notice how Mary elaborated on the attributes of God in her song. She spoke of His might, His personal involvement in her life, His holiness, His mercy. She pointed to His mighty works and His kindness to His own. She concluded with lingering notes of His faithfulness to keep His promises.

Mary's joy was firmly rooted in the faithfulness of God. She knew Him. She rejoiced in Him.

Sometimes we stagger in hopelessness because we forget who God is.

We believe He has forsaken or forgotten us…in spite of His clear promise, "I will never leave thee, nor forsake thee" (Hebrews 13:5).

We believe He cannot help us…in spite of the fact that He upholds "all things by the word of his power" (Hebrews 1:3).

We believe He does not care for us…in spite of His offer to cast "all your care upon him; for he careth for you" (1 Peter 5:7).

We believe He will not sustain us…in spite of His commitment that He "giveth power to the faint; and to them that have no might he increaseth strength" (Isaiah 40:29).

We believe we are beyond the reach of His comfort… in spite of His claim to be "the God of all comfort; Who comforteth us in all our tribulation" (2 Corinthians 1:3–4).

Simply put, what we believe about God is not true. No wonder joy eludes us! We have forgotten who our God is and what He desires to do in our lives.

Philippians 4:4 instructs, "Rejoice in the Lord alway: and again I say, Rejoice." We cannot always rejoice in our circumstances. But we can always rejoice in the Lord. With Christ as our Saviour, we have an endless supply of reasons to rejoice.

Consider this partial list of what Jesus is for us, and remember, it is only a beginning!

He is our:

- Counselor (Isaiah 9:6)
- Deliverer (Romans 11:26)
- Redeemer (Isaiah 47:4)
- Saviour (Isaiah 45:21)
- Friend (John 15:14–15)

- Shepherd (Hebrews 13:20)
- Guide (Psalm 48:14)
- Everlasting Father (Isaiah 9:6)
- Prince of Peace (Isaiah 9:6)
- Author and finisher of our faith (Hebrews 12:2)
- Blessed hope (Titus 2:13)
- Creator (John 1:3)
- Bread of life (John 6:35)
- Sustainer (Psalm 55:22)
- Refuge (Psalm 46:1)
- Strength (Philippians 4:13)
- Light of life (John 8:12)
- Source of truth (John 14:6)

Regardless of how black the night, Jesus never changes. His love is constant, and His faithfulness is unending. In our darkest hours, we may not be able to discern all of His qualities, but we can trust them. And we can rejoice in them.

Months before the first Christmas, Mary chose joy by basing her belief in God's Word. Rather than dwelling on the aspects of her situation that would cause grief, she meditated on God's faithfulness and chose to rejoice in Him!

We unwrap the joys of a Christmas night when we sing praise to our God.

WE REJOICE IN GOD'S GLORY

The second "Christmas carol" recorded in Scripture was sung by the angels themselves. I would have loved to have been there to hear their songs of praise reverberate through the otherwise quiet, lonely hills.

And there were in the same country shepherds abiding in the field, keeping watch over their flock by night. And, lo, the angel of the Lord came upon them, and the glory of the Lord shone round about them: and they were sore afraid. And the angel said unto them, Fear not: for, behold, I bring you good tidings of great joy, which shall be to all people. For unto you is born this day in the city of David a Saviour, which is Christ the Lord. And this shall be a sign unto you;

*Ye shall find the babe wrapped in swaddling clothes,
lying in a manger. And suddenly there was with the
angel a multitude of the heavenly host praising God,
and saying, Glory to God in the highest, and on earth
peace, good will toward men.*—LUKE 2:8–14

Like Mary, the angels centered their message on
Jesus. But they ended with a special refrain, sung by a full
angelic choir, magnifying the glory of God.

It must have been incredible for the angels to watch
their Creator humble Himself and enter Earth through
a virgin's womb. It must have been amazing to them to
observe His choice to be born in a manger and wrapped
in simple swaddling clothes. After all, they knew exactly
who Jesus was—the "Saviour, which is Christ the Lord"
(Luke 2:11).

Yet the angels observed the unfolding events of
Christmas from a different perspective than anyone on
earth. You see, the angels live to bring glory and praise
to God, and they do it continually around His throne. So
when they announced the Christmas story, it was second

nature for them to rejoice in God's glory manifested through His grace.

In Revelation 5:12, the angels are part of a choir who praise God for His wondrous and merciful plan of redemption. Once again, they are rejoicing in God's glory: "Worthy is the Lamb that was slain to receive power, and riches, and wisdom, and strength, and honour, and glory, and blessing."

When we remember the Christmas story, we often think only of the manger, the shepherds, the stable—the characters and events of that special night. But when the angels announced the Christmas story, they saw a bigger picture. And they rejoiced in how that night was woven by God into His eternal purposes of redemption.

Just as the chords of Mary's song sweetly celebrated the truth that Christ's presence brings joy in the night, the anthem of the angels featured another avenue of joy. The angels' message tells us that remembering God's eternal purposes through our lives brings us joy.

One of the most oft-claimed promises in all of Scripture is Romans 8:28: "And we know that all things work together for good to them that love God, to them who are the called according to his purpose." We prize this verse because it assures us that God is able to take even the worst moments of our lives and redeem them for our good.

But notice in the next two verses the process that brings all of this about: "For whom he did foreknow, he also did predestinate to be conformed to the image of his Son, that he might be the firstborn among many brethren. Moreover whom he did predestinate, them he also called: and whom he called, them he also justified: and whom he justified, them he also glorified."

In God's sovereignty, He is able to take the night seasons of our lives and use them to conform us to the image of Christ! Through this process, God is glorified, and we are fulfilled, for we become the people that God created us to be.

Of course, it's difficult in the middle of the night to see how this works. Our minds are so predisposed to believing joy comes from comfort and pleasure that in moments of pain, we forget to look for God's hand of sovereignty. The angels' nighttime carol teaches us that during night seasons we can rejoice in knowing that God's glory will be made manifest through His eternal purposes.

Second Corinthians 4:17–18 encourages us to look at the big picture during night seasons: "For our light affliction, which is but for a moment, worketh for us a far more exceeding and eternal weight of glory; While we look not at the things which are seen, but at the things which are not seen: for the things which are seen are temporal; but the things which are not seen are eternal."

Trusting that God has a bigger purpose in mind than we can see or understand brings great joy—even in the night.

WE REJOICE IN GOD'S SALVATION

Everyone seems to view the Christmas story from a different vantage point. Little Chloe, as she unpacked the family nativity set, said aloud the name of each figure she unwrapped from its newspaper and set on the table. "Here's the donkey, here's Mary, here's the shepherd, here's the angel, here's baby Jesus in His car seat...."

I suppose a manger could look like a unique car seat to a twenty-first century American four year old; but the shepherds knew exactly what it was. And they were amazed to see Christ—God in the flesh—resting His infant head in a manger.

The shepherds were privileged to be firsthand witnesses of Christmas. With their own eyes they saw Jesus lying in the straw with Mary and Joseph hovering over Him. With their own ears they heard the angels announce that this was indeed God in the flesh.

What would you do if you saw the first manger scene?

The shepherds knew exactly what to do! "And when they had seen it, they made known abroad the saying which was told them concerning this child" (Luke 2:17). They told their story to everyone who would listen.

That night had been the most eventful of their lives. They had experienced an emotional roller coaster of fear, excitement, surprise, shock, and amazement. But when the night was over, they "returned, glorifying and praising God for all the things that they had heard and seen" (Luke 2:20).

Aside from Mary and Joseph, the shepherds had been the first to hear the good news that Christ the Saviour was born. They had been the first to see Him—right there in front of their eyes. And now, in their rejoicing, they couldn't help but share the glad tidings with others.

The rejoicing of the shepherds teaches us that when our night season is past, we have opportunity (and responsibility) to share with others the joy God gave us through the night. For as we experience the faithfulness of God in the night and learn to rejoice in His glory, we find that God truly does reward faith with a joyous end.

Hours earlier, at the instruction of angels, the shepherds had quite uncharacteristically left their sheep alone on the hillside. Their journey to the manger began in faith, and it ended in praise.

And so it is for us. Our journey to God begins in faith as we receive the gift of His salvation (see page 119). But it will end in perfect praise when we enter His presence with rejoicing.

But our rejoicing does not begin at the end. All throughout the journey, as we walk by faith in His Word, we can rejoice in His salvation. Even as the shepherds "made known abroad the saying which was told them concerning this child," we can also testify of our personal experience of God's sustaining grace. There is no joy quite like that of relating the goodness of God to others.

Christmas is a time for rejoicing! Even in the night seasons, we can express the joy of the Lord when we look to His faithfulness, rejoice in His glory, and share His goodness with others.

Christmas night delivered God's greatest gift to the world. And those who were first privileged to discover this gift unwrapped it with joy. Their songs remind us that even in night seasons—especially in night seasons—we can express the joy of Christmas.

Conclusion
THE GIFT OF ANTICIPATION

You'll never meet a more enthusiastic gift-giver than my younger daughter, Kristine. One of the most delightful possessions in our home, in fact, is a permanent documentation of Kristine's gift-giving exuberance on a family movie. There's a ninety-second segment of this old VHS that, as a family, we love to rewind and watch over and over.

Three-year-old Matthew was going through a rootin' tootin' cowboy phase in his life, and he loved western paraphernalia. Terrie and I bought him a pair of cowboy boots, and we let Kristine, who was five at the time, in on the secret. We saved the special boots until the end, and Kristine was bursting with excitement for her little brother, because she knew he was going to love those cowboy boots. We had, naturally, cautioned Kristine not to tell Matt what the gift was, and she had kept the secret very well. But it was almost more than she could handle.

Our video shows Kristine excitedly giving Matthew the box to open and then hovering over him to watch. Her entire body was quivering with anticipation.

Just before Matt began to tear the paper, Kristine crowded in closer and asked in a high-pitched, very-excited-little-girl trill, "Do you know what it is, Matt?"

As Matt tore the first corner of the wrapping, it became too much for little Kristine. She could not contain her joy one second longer. "BOOTS!!! It's boots, Matthew!!!!"

To this day, when we gather to open gifts as a family, someone is sure to tease Kristine, "It's boots!"

Christmas is an incredible gift. As we unwrap it, we find it is the kind of gift we've always wanted. It contains the love of God delivered through Christ. Through Christmas, we have Christ's presence here with us. We gain His peace and learn His joy.

But I have to tell you: unwrapping Christmas is like just tearing the first corner off a larger gift. Christ's first coming in the manger isn't the end of the story; it's not the full gift.

As we discover Christ's love through Christmas, He leans in close and says, "But do you really know what this means? Do you understand what this gift is?" And before we can even fully unwrap it, He joyfully says, "It's your promise that I'm coming again!!!!"

It's boots, Matthew!

It's the return of Christ, Christian!

Scripture is full of promises concerning Christ's coming to Earth, many of them made hundreds of years before He was born. But only some of these promises were fulfilled through Christmas. From His birth in the manger to His resurrection, some scholars estimate that Christ fulfilled over *three hundred* prophecies. Here are just a few:

- Born of a virgin (Isaiah 7:14; Matthew 1:20–23)
- From the house of Judah (Isaiah 37:31; Matthew 1:1–2)
- From the house of David (Isaiah 16:5; Matthew 1:1, 6, 16)
- Born in Bethlehem Ephrathah (Micah 5:2; Matthew 2:1)
- From Nazareth of Galilee (Isaiah 9:1–2; Matthew 2:22–23, Matthew 4:13–16)
- Would come out of Egypt (Hosea 11:1; Matthew 2:14–15)
- Mission would include the Gentiles (Isaiah 49:6, Isaiah 42:1–6; Matthew 12:14–21)
- Ministry would include miraculous healings (Isaiah 29:18, Isaiah 35:5–6; Luke 7:20–22)
- Ministry would deliver spiritual captives (Isaiah 61:1–2; Luke 4:16–21)
- Despised and rejected by men (Isaiah 53:3; Matthew 26:57–27:50)
- Hated without cause (Psalm 69:4; Isaiah 49:7; John 15:24–25)

- Betrayed for thirty pieces of silver (Zechariah 11:12; Matthew 26:14–15)
- Beaten with a rod (Micah 5:1; Mark 15:19)
- Given vinegar and gall to drink (Psalm 69:21; Matthew 27:34, 48)
- Hands and feet nailed (Psalm 22:16; John 20:25)
- Buried in a rich man's tomb (Isaiah 53:9; Matthew 27:57–60)
- Rose from the dead (Isaiah 53:8–11; Matthew 28:2–9)

But the prophecies of Christ's first coming aren't the only ones in Scripture. Bible scholars have counted more than 1,480 scriptural references to His Second Coming. Because of the fulfilled promises of Christ's first coming, we can confidently anticipate His Second Coming!

For the Lord himself shall descend from heaven with a shout, with the voice of the archangel, and with the trump of God: and the dead in Christ shall rise first: Then we which are alive and remain shall be caught up together with them in the clouds, to meet the

Lord in the air: and so shall we ever be with the Lord.
—1 THESSALONIANS 4:16–17

When I was a little boy, I had the terrible habit of trying to figure out what my Christmas presents were. I would feel, shake, and even try to peek into the packages. One year, I felt what I was pretty sure was a BB gun. I didn't unwrap it, but I did play with it while it was still in the package. When no one was around, I would hold it to my shoulder and shoot imaginary targets in the living room.

In reality, I was enjoying the pleasures of a future event. The package had my name on it. I knew what it was. And I knew I would love it. But only Christmas morning would reveal its fullness.

So it is with the gift of Christ's presence. Christmas is our promise that Christ is coming again to establish a kingdom in which pain, suffering, and all sorrow will be gone forever. Sin and Satan will be vanquished. War and strife will be forgotten, while peace and goodwill toward men will be the glad reality in every heart. We will live in the untarnished joy of Christ's direct presence. It's hard to imagine a gift greater than Christmas, but Christ's eternal kingdom is just that.

Until then, unwrapping Christmas is the opportunity to enjoy the promise of Christ's coming kingdom even now. It's a taste of the greater pleasures of the future. Christ first came to Earth as a humble baby. But when He returns, He will come as our glorious King.

The love of Christ that we unwrap through Christmas is greater than we will fully experience in our entire lifespan. But as we unwrap it, God gives us another gift—the anticipation of His glorious kingdom.

Indeed, Christmas is a gift.

One Final Word

A GIFT MUST BE RECEIVED

Throughout these pages, we've looked at unwrapping the gift of Christmas. But have you ever considered that a gift must be *received* before it can be *unwrapped*? And have you ever received the gift of Christmas?

Let me explain: Christ came to Earth over two thousand years ago so we could know the reality of His presence in our lives—just as we've seen in this book. But before we can discover what His presence can mean in our everyday lives, we must first receive Him personally.

When Christ came to Earth, most rejected Him. John 1:11 records, "He came unto his own, and his own received him not." As Jesus ministered, some ridiculed Him, some doubted His claim to be the Son of God, and even the religious leaders of His day rejected Him. They were too proud to admit that they needed Him—that their own man-made systems of religion were not sufficient to gain eternal life.

But, some received Christ. John 1 continues, "But as many as received him, to them gave he power to become the sons of God, even to them that believe on his name" (John 1:12).

Many people—religious and non-religious alike—have misconceptions of what it means to receive Christ and His salvation. Some believe we know God through our lineage—being "born into a Christian family." Others believe we earn a relationship with God through good works, such as kindness to others, involvement in a church, or moral living. Still others believe it has nothing to do with religion and that God only judges the sincerity of our hearts. They maintain that if we are sincere and consistent in our chosen belief system, He will overlook our faults.

But Christ Himself made the truth very clear—and very simple. He said a relationship with God and salvation from sin is a gift—and, as a gift, it must be received.

So, as we conclude this small book, I'd like to ask you to take a few moments to understand what it means to *receive* Christ personally.

Let's start at the beginning...

WHY YOU MUST RECEIVE THIS GIFT

The Bible is very clear that we all have a huge problem—sin. In fact, our sin is the reason Christ came to Earth. We were all born with a sin nature that separates us from God. Romans 3:23 explains, "For all have sinned, and come short of the glory of God." Even the best of us are sinners.

Sin has a high price tag, too. Romans 6:23 says, "For the wages of sin is death...." In other words, the price for sin is eternal death apart from God in a lake of fire called Hell. Revelation 21:8 describes this place and those who go there: "But the fearful, and unbelieving, and the abominable, and murderers, and whoremongers, and sorcerers, and idolaters, and all liars, shall have their part in the lake which burneth with fire and brimstone: which is the second death." Literally, this is where sinners (like you and me) are headed apart from the miracle of Christ and what He provided for us.

And that is what Christmas is all about. Jesus didn't come just so we would have a sweet story about God coming to us and being born in a manger. Mark 10:45 tells us, "the Son of man came...to give his life a ransom for many."

HOW JESUS PURCHASED OUR GIFT

As we saw a moment ago, the payment for our sin is death, but in God's great mercy, Jesus made that payment for us. The rest of Romans 6:23 says, "...but the gift of God is eternal life through Jesus Christ our Lord." Again in Romans 5:8 God says, "But God commendeth [proved] his love toward us, in that, while we were yet sinners, Christ died for us."

Jesus Christ came to earth as God in the flesh, lived a perfect life, and then voluntarily died on a cross because He loves you. On that cross, He literally paid for all of your sins. He took your blame! He punished Himself for your sin. Then, because He is God, He rose from the dead three days later and now offers you the gift of salvation. What a great gift!

John 3:16 says, "For God so loved the world, that he gave his only begotten Son, that whosoever believeth in him should not perish, but have everlasting life." God, in His awesome love, came to earth to make a way for you to be forgiven of your sins and given eternal life!

HOW YOU CAN RECEIVE HIS GIFT

Salvation is a gift—purchased by Christ. *Knowing* Jesus died to pay for our sins is not enough; we must choose to *believe* and *receive* His gift. Romans 10:13 says, "For whosoever shall call upon the name of the Lord shall be saved." In verse 10 of that same chapter, God says, "For with the heart man believeth unto righteousness; and with the mouth confession is made unto salvation." It's as simple as believing what God says and then choosing to receive His gift!

If you've never asked Jesus Christ to be your personal Saviour, you could do that right now. Simply confess to Him that you understand you are a sinner deserving of Hell and that you trust His payment for your forgiveness and salvation. You could sincerely pray something like this:

> *Lord Jesus, I believe that You are God, that You died for my sin, and that You rose again from the dead. I know that I am a sinner, and I ask You now to be my personal Saviour. I'm placing my full trust in You alone, and I now accept Your gift of eternal life. Thank You for keeping Your promise!*

This is the gift of Christmas! Christ came to redeem us from our sins and to restore our relationship with God.

It is only after you receive Christ that you can truly begin to unwrap His infinite love.

If you have just chosen to receive Christ's gift, we would love to hear from you! Please send an email to Christmasgift@strivingtogether.com. Additionally, you will find resources and Bible messages to help you grow in your relationship with God at our website: dailyintheword.org.

ABOUT THE AUTHOR

PAUL CHAPPELL is the senior pastor of Lancaster Baptist Church and president of West Coast Baptist College in Lancaster, California. His biblical vision has led the church to become one of the most dynamic Baptist churches in the nation. His preaching is heard on Daily in the Word, a daily radio broadcast heard across America. Pastor Chappell has four children who are married and serving in Christian ministry. He has been married to his wife Terrie for over thirty years.

Connect with Paul Chappell at PaulChappell.com

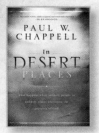

Visit us online

strivingtogether.com

wcbc.edu